TRAPPED IN DEVIL'S HOLE

AS TOLD TO BEN EAST

ILLUSTRATED & DESIGNED BY JACK DAHL

EDITED BY JEROLYN NENTL AND DR. HOWARD SCHROEDER

Professor in Reading and Language Arts, Dept. of Elementary Education, Mankato State University

Library of Congress Cataloging in Publication Data

East, Ben.
 Trapped in devil's hole, as told to Ben East.
 SUMMARY: In hopes of doing their best trout fishing ever, two men in-
stead become injured and stranded in the gorge of a dangerous river.
 1. Trout fishing--Juvenile literature. 2. Wilderness survival--Juvenile
literature. (1. Fishing. 2. Wilderness survival. 3. Survival) I. Dahl, John I. II.
Nentl, Jerolyn Ann. III. Schroeder, Howard. IV. Title. V. Series.
SH687.E27   799.1'7'55   79-53773
ISBN 0-89686-048-5 lib. bdg.
ISBN 0-89686-056-6 pbk.

International Standard Book Numbers:	Library of Congress
0-89686-048-5 Library Bound	**Catalog Number:**
0-89686-056-6 Paperback	79-53773

Adapted from the original publication *Survival* by **Outdoor Life,**
Copyright 1967.

CRESTWOOD HOUSE

P.O. Box 3427
Hwy. 66 South
Mankato, MN 56001

ABOUT THE AUTHOR...

Ben East has been an *Outdoor Life* staff editor since 1946. Born in south-eastern Michigan in 1898, and a lifelong resident of that state, he sold his first story to *Outers Recreation* (later absorbed by *Outdoor Life*) in 1921. In 1926 he began a career as a professional writer, becoming outdoor editor of Booth Newspapers, a chain of dailies in eight major Michigan cities outside Detroit.

He left the newspaper job on January 1, 1946, to become Midwest field editor of Outdoor Life. In 1966 he was advanced to senior field editor, a post from which he retired at the end of 1970. Since then he has continued to write for the magazine as a contributing field editor.

Growing up as a farm boy, he began fishing and hunting as soon as he could handle a cane pole and a .22 rifle. He has devoted sixty years to outdoor sports, travel, adventure, wildlife photography, writing and lecturing. Ben has covered much of the back country of North America, from the eastern seaboard to the Aleutian Islands of Alaska, and from the Canadian arctic to the southern United States. He has written more than one thousand magazine articles and eight books. Today his by-line is one of the best known of any outdoor writer in the country. His outstanding achievement in wildlife photography was the making of the first color film ever taken of the Alaskan sea otter, in the summer of 1941.

In recent years much of his writing has dealt with major conservation problems confronting the nation. He has produced hard-hitting and effective articles on such environmentally destructive practices as strip mining, channelization, unethical use of aircraft to take trophy game, political interference in wildlife affairs, the indiscriminate use of pesticides and the damming of wild and scenic rivers and streams.

In 1973, he was signally honored when the Michigan Senate and House of Representatives adopted a concurrent resolution, the legislature's highest tribute, recognizing him for his distinguished contribution to the conservation of natural resources.

A FOREWORD TO TRAPPED IN DEVIL'S HOLE

As the readers of this story will discover, Keith Oveson and John McClary were in great danger in the Devil's Hole. Even those, who were trying to rescue them, were not all sure the men could be brought out alive. Had it not been for the great courage and skill of a few men trained in rescue work, the story certainly would have had an unhappy ending.

The story appeared in newspapers in every part of the country. By reading that story I learned of the two fishermen's dangerous ordeal.

It was part of my job, as a field editor of Outdoor Life magazine, to check out such stories. I was to make sure they were true, and with the help of the persons involved, write the stories for the magazine. That was how I got to know these two men.

Their story had an interesting and exciting follow-up. In one of our phone talks, Keith Oveson said that shortly before he and his partner had been trapped in the Devil's Hole, there had been a bad case of rattlesnake bite in that same area. I began at once to track down the story.

After three or four tries, I found the snakebite victim. He was Daniel Utt, a forty-two year-old California oil company superintendent. With a partner and his twelve year-old son, he made a pack trip to the San Joaquin, two miles above the Devil's Hole. Then he sent the guide and pack horses back, planning to stay for four days of fishing.

Walking to the river from their camp in midafternoon, Utt was struck just above the ankle by a large Pacific rattler. Other fishermen from a nearby camp went for help. It was eighteen hours before a helicopter flew in to take Daniel Utt to a hospital. He faced death every minute of that eighteen hours.

In the end he survived, but his leg had to be removed above the knee. He was the third man to escape death in the canyon of the San Joaquin.

BEN EAST

Keith Oveson and John McClary stood on the trail that ran along the rim of the gorge. The Middle Fork of the San Joaquin River tumbled down its canyon one thousand feet below them. It looked like a twisting, silver snake. Patches of green and blue glistened in the sun.

They were trout fishermen. Below them was water they had never before fished. John thought perhaps no one had ever fished there. It was too hard to reach. Just the sight of it made their hearts skip a beat!

They were in the wild and rugged country of the Sierra Nevadas in west-central California. Yosemite National Park was to the northeast. It was midmorning, but the canyon was still in deep shadow. The walls were smooth and bare. They dropped in steep slopes from one ledge to another. There was an occasional clump of manzanita and mountain mahogony. Some sparse grass grew out of the crevices.

Keith and John were both thinking about a route to the bottom. Neither had any climbing experience. They eyed the pitch of the slides and the height of the low cliffs where the ledges fell away. It was going to be a tough climb, but they were sure they could make it. They were eager to enjoy three leisurely days at their favorite sport this Labor Day weekend.

7

John had stopped by to visit Keith one night in February. He had found him busily tying a fly at his workbench. He watched him for a moment and finally said:

"Man, I know a place where you could have a ball with that."

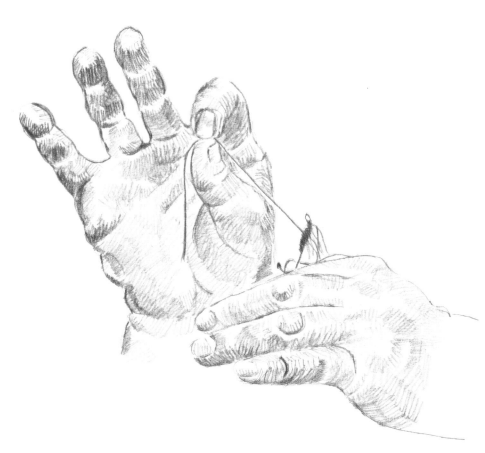

Keith knew quite a few places where he could "have a ball" with the flies he was tying. But no fisherman ever passes up a chance to hear about a new fishing hole.

"Where?" he asked.

"The gorge of the San Joaquin," John said. "A spot I call the Devil's Hole. You can fish below it and above it. But there's about a half mile of deep gorge that nobody gets into. It's virgin water. From what I've caught downstream, it's got to be crawling with trout."

Six months of hoping for and planning had followed that winter night. Now they stood on the brink of what they hoped would be the best trout fishing ever.

The men knew they were going into remote country. They had chosen their outfits with great care. They wanted to keep the weight of their backpacks as light as possible. They took food, a frying pan, GI mess kits and canteens. They also took snake and first aid kits, knives and waterproof matches. A light ax, mending kit and tape, string, a survival kit and thirty feet of nylon parachute cord were also packed. They took no tent.

They left home late Friday and drove to the Clover Meadow ranger station. It was an hour after midnight when they arrived. They camped for the night, and would leave their car there.

The next morning Keith made breakfast while John went to talk with the ranger, Virgil Bishop. The two men planned to be out of the canyon by Monday noon, Labor Day. Ranger Bishop asked that they check in at the station before leaving for home. He wanted to be sure they had made it safely.

The men had hiked three miles from the ranger station to this spot on the rim where they were viewing the river. It had been a good trail and they made it in about an hour. Now they were taking a few moments rest before starting the climb into the gorge.

The first few hundred feet down were fairly easy. They were on crumbling granite and it felt like very coarse sand through their boots. They half slid and half lowered themselves. Then the "sand" turned into loose rock and the going got tougher.

The sun was high now and it was hot. The climb was hard work. Keith had an old knee injury from a flying accident during World War II that bothered him. It was harder for him to climb downhill than uphill. They scrambled and fought their way down the canyon wall. Their packs felt heavier and heavier all the time.

The first hint of trouble came when they were about halfway down the canyon. It was not serious, but it was a warning if they heeded it.

Their feet began to hurt.

In another half hour, Keith's toes were burning. John was suffering even more. When they stopped on a ledge to check what was wrong, they found they both had bad blisters. John's were broken and raw. His boots had just been repaired and had been resewn too tightly. Rough seams had been left on the inside. The two men applied salve and bandages and continued their descent.

The canyon wall changed now. The broken ledges and sparse brush became bare granite. Water from centuries ago had worn it smooth. The men fell back on their parachute cord. In the worst places, they lowered first their packs and then themselves. They had to feel for toe and finger holds in the few crevices. They were straining and sweating, and a little scared. Finally, they reached the river.

It had been six hours since they had left the rim. It was the hardest six hours either of them had ever put in on a fishing trip. Their blistered feet felt like they were on fire. As they looked around, they still thought it had been worth it.

The San Joaquin is a clear stream of medium size in late summer. There are deep black pools and pockets of slow current. But there are also rapids foaming around the rocks and boulders. Never had they seen more tempting water!

Before the men could start fishing, they knew they had to take care of their feet. They lugged their packs to a sandbar and pulled off their boots. The bandages they had put on had rubbed off. The blisters were now worn to bleeding sores. They dressed them as best they could.

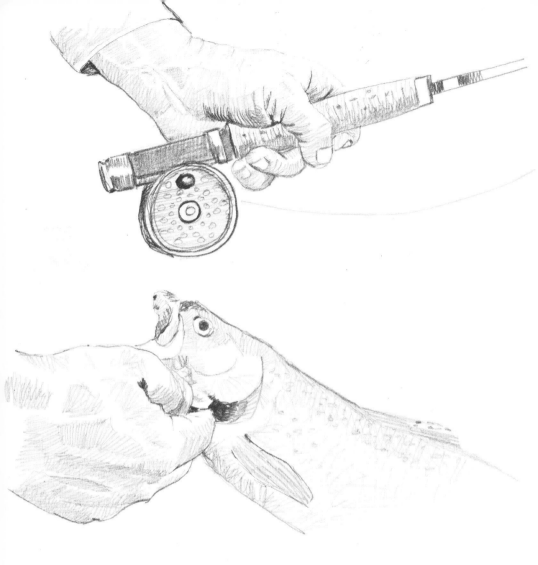

Then they put their fishing rods together. Trout were feeding in the pool below the sandbar. Now and then they could see fish drift out from hiding places to snatch bits of food. It was a trout fisherman's paradise!

Soon they had caught enough for supper. The sun was hidden by the high cliffs now. Shadows were beginning to deepen in the canyon.

Before the men lit a fire, they took off their boots once more. John was in real trouble now. His feet were swollen so badly he could not get on his boots. Keith had packed in a pair of sneakers for wading and John put them on. Keith wore a size 10, John a 6$^1/_2$, but they would have to do.

For the first time, the two men began to worry a little. They discussed the climb back up the wall. They admitted it would be suicide to tackle the granite face with their feet in the shape they were.

The men knew the canyon opened upstream around a sharp bend in the river. They had seen a fisherman in a pool there while climbing down the canyon wall. But they were blocked from going in that direction. Straight cliffs rising two hundred feet from the water were between them and that pool.

Downstream a half mile or so, they knew there was a camp at Granite Creek Falls. There was a steep trail angling up from the river at the campsite. John had been there four or five times. They would have no trouble climbing out if they could reach that trail. But they had no way of knowing what obstacles lay in the gorge between them and the camp. They could not see around the first bend in the river.

The problems were many, but they agreed to put their worries aside until morning. They lit their fire and ate a good supper of trout, bread and jam, cheese and coffee. They told stories about past fishing trips until the fire died. Then it was time to crawl into their sleeping bags.

Looking up out of that gorge was like looking out of a giant well. It was inky black all around. Just a strip of sky ablaze with stars could be seen overhead.

Dawn was creeping down the canyon walls when they awoke. The only sound at daybreak was the rush and tumble of the river. There were few birds in the gorge. It seemed an eerie place at that hour of the day, and not too cheerful. They talked things over bluntly while they cooked breakfast.

Keith had grown up in ranch country in the southeast corner of Utah. Self-reliance is taken for granted there. He had fished in most of the famous rivers in the West. He had floated the whitewater of several rivers. John was younger and had less experience, but he was cool and a levelheaded thinker.

The men knew they were in a tight spot. Still, they were confident they could get themselves out of it. One thing was certain. They had to forget about any more fishing and start at once.

So they cooked the five eggs that were left and some more trout and fried a can of potatoes. They would start with full stomaches.

Keith and John began by scouting upstream. That way out was blocked, just as they had figured the night before. Then Keith came up with a plan. He had experience running fast water in rubber rafts. He proposed that they could float their packs and swim the series of pools downstream to the Granite Creek Falls Camp. They could climb over any rocks that blocked their way.

There would be some risk, of course. Keith had not forgotten the whirlpools of rivers he had been on in the past. He had even been carried over falls once or twice. He knew the terrible power of the water. John was a good swimmer, but he had never tackled fast current. Still, he was game to try.

With a little luck, they felt they could reach the Granite Creek Falls by nightfall. Then they could have all Monday to climb out of the canyon and hike back to their car. That would put them home on schedule. Their families would not become alarmed.

19

The two men sorted their gear. They left everything but the bare essentials. They kept the mess kits, canteens, ax, frying pan, sleeping bags and fishing gear. Food would be no problem if they were going to get out of the canyon by the next day. So they took only four slices of bacon, half a loaf of bread, a small piece of cheese, a can of stew, a box of cookies, enough coffee for four cups, and some lemon juice.

They found three pieces of driftwood long enough to go under both air mattresses. Then they lashed the makeshift raft together with string. It was frail, but it was the best they could do. They tied the parachute cord to the raft and loaded the packs. The men led the raft down through the first pool. They walked and waded along the shore. The water was not deep, but it was as cold as liquid ice.

At the end of the pool, the river forked around some big rocks. Then it plunged through white-water chutes barely wide enough to take the raft. The men carried the packs up over a ledge. John rode the raft through to keep it from hanging up on the rocks. Keith kept it in check with the cord. John had almost made it to the bottom, lying flat across the two mattresses. But suddenly he bounced against a rock and hung in the raging current, just about to capsize! Water was pouring over the raft. He hung on, and finally found footing.

The men had met their first taste of the terrible force of the river!

Looking back upstream, they could see they had come no more than one hundred yards. But they had been in and out of the water for two hours. It was going to be slow going.

The next pool ended in a jumble of rocks. The two men scouted around for quite awhile. Finally they found a huge slab of granite two hundred feet tall. It had broken away from the wall without falling over. At the bottom was an opening just wide enough for a man. They carried their packs and the raft through the damp, cold crevice.

Back in the sunlight again, they found a big U-shaped bend in the river. Here the water ran deep. It also ran slick against the face of an overhanging cliff. It was the most dangerous spot so far.

It was also the point of no return. Once they were around that bend, there would be no hope of coming back.

The pool was so deep it was jet black. The river swept them in under the overhang. Keith felt the current tugging his legs toward the rock wall, drawing him down. He could see nothing in the dark water. The river seemed to be pouring through a cleft or into an underground cave. He kicked hard to get back to the surface, catching John on the knee. He felt his foot against the wall and pushed away! It was their first close call.

Just below the bend was a sandbar where they could rest. They gathered a few pieces of driftwood, heated their one can of stew and ate a little cheese. It was a meager lunch. Keith and John did not know it then, but it was to be the best meal they would have for four days.

That afternoon the two men found a series of narrow ledges just above the water. Following them around a bend, they looked straight down the gorge at the Granite Creek Falls Camp. It was only five hundred yards away!

"We've got it made," Keith cried. "We'll be there before dark." But before he said it, he knew he had spoken too soon. They could hear the roar of a waterfall downstream. At that point the river disappeared. The Canyon walls dropped vertically to the brink of the water on both sides.

There were only two hours of daylight left. The two men used the time in a heartbreaking struggle

to reach a flat table rock at the very top of the falls
so they could look over. They never made it. But
they got close enough to see that the river swirled
into its plunge in a wicked whirlpool. Then it nar-
rowed and knifed through a deep slot. Spray was
flying high in the air. The drop of the water sounded
like thunder. No swimmer could hope of going over
the falls and live.

27

Here, within sight of their goal, they finally had to face the bitter truth. They were hopelessly trapped. They could not get past the waterfall. There was no way to go back upstream. Their blistered feet prevented them from climbing the granite walls of the gorge, even if they could have found a route.

Keith and John had been wading, swimming, climbing and carrying their packs for thirteen hours. Both men were exhausted. They spent the night on three big boulders wedged in midstream. They found enough driftwood for a small fire, but they went without supper. Neither man seemed to care. They huddled in their sleeping bags for warmth and tried to make light of their troubles. But they did not sleep much that night.

The trapped men were in no real danger, but they could be in serious trouble soon. They were short of food and did not think a helicopter could get low enough for a rescue. It seemed doubtful even rescuers could lead them back up the walls because of their blistered feet.

Keith and John knew they would not be missed for another twenty-four hours. They had told their families they would be home Monday night. Keith's wife had waited for her husband many times. She would not worry. But the men knew if they were not home by Tuesday morning, she and John's wife would sound an alarm.

Monday morning, the trapped men ate very little. All they had was a small piece of cheese, a cup of weak coffee and two cookies apiece. They roped themselves together with the parachute cord. Then they set out to go back upstream. At the last sandbar they had seen, there was a break in the cliff. Cedar trees grew there. The cedar meant firewood and smoke signals. Ranger Bishop had told them to make smoke signals if they needed help. They would camp on that sandbar until they were rescued.

All that day, they tested the wall, looking vainly for a route up to the rim. They went without lunch. Supper was no better than breakfast. At dark, they stashed the bacon and cheese that remained in a small cave, since it looked like rain.

31

Tuesday morning they awoke to find their food gone. A squirrel or pack rat must have carried it off during the night. But their thoughts were on making smoke signals, not eating. Keith and John piled up green cedar branches for a driftwood fire. Then they lit the fire during a lull between winds. There is a lull after the cooler, nighttime wind blowing downstream dies and before the warmer daytime wind begins blowing upstream. The fire sent up a column of dense white smoke. But the smoke drifted away in the air currents before it reached the rim.

That morning the men went fishing for the first time since Saturday. They soon caught their breakfast. There was no fat for frying, but they learned to put a little water in the mess kits. Steaming the fish worked just fine. At least they would not go hungry.

There was nothing to do now but wait. Their blistered feet made movement painful. They fished the rest of Tuesday and on Wednesday, while eating a late lunch, three shots rang out from on top of the rim! They dropped their mess kits and raced for lookout rock in the river. At the top of the canyon the form of a man was seen against the sky. He looked about the size of a doll.

They waved wildly! After a minute, the tiny figure waved back.

They had been found!

The man on the rim was a friend of John's. He was one of many friends and relatives who joined in the search for the two lost men. Their wives had called the search when they did not return home by Tuesday, just as the men had expected.

Half an hour later they heard a helicopter. Then a big, silver Air Force chopper came into sight around the bend downstream. It flew up the canyon. Then it turned and flew back. A man standing in the door tossed out a message wrapped around a stick.

"Stay put," it read. "Help is on the way."

But there was no further sign of rescue until Thursday afternoon. Then men showed up at the Granite Creek Falls Camp. Two of them in swimming trunks worked their way up the river. They got close enough to wave at the trapped men. But they could not get past the waterfall. After an hour or so, they gave up and went back.

Late that day, the unhappy men heard the helicopter again. They had spelled out F-O-O-D with green branches on the sandbar. The men in the chopper tossed out two cans on the first pass. They fell into the river. Their aim was better on the second pass. A tin of jam and biscuits almost fell into Keith's pocket. On the third run, the chopper banked and dropped a full box of rations. It was tied to a sheet to check its fall. It hit the rocks and broke open. But most of the tins were not damaged. That night they ate their first real meal since Sunday morning.

Nothing else happened until Friday afternoon. About 3:30 p.m. the two men were sitting beside their small fire on the sandbar when a voice said "Hello!" They looked up to see Virgil Bishop, the Clover Meadow ranger, walking out of the cedars. His helper, Murray Taylor, was with him. They had been fighting their way down the canyon wall since 6:30 a.m.

Bishop had been off duty because of illness in his family. He did not know the two men were missing until Thursday. When he took a look at their feet, he agreed. Rescue would not be as simple as climbing back up the wall.

"An Air Force rescue team is on the way," he said. "It would be best to wait for them."

Taylor stayed to help. Bishop started back up the wall. It made Keith and John unhappy to watch Bishop climb, but know they could not follow!

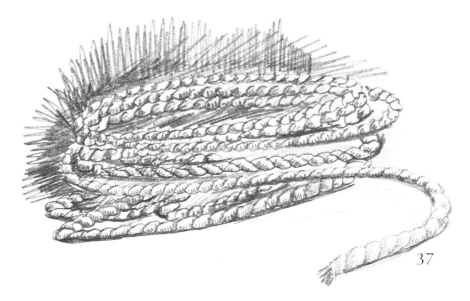

Meanwhile, a top rescue and survival man was going into action. He was T/Sgt. Anthony Martino, a veteran paramedic. He headed the river survival course at the Hamilton Airbase. He was an icy-nerved climber and jumper. For this rescue, Martino had a helper. He was Lt. Tom Finan, a mountain rescue expert.

By nightfall they were halfway down the wall. They spent the night on a ledge. By morning they had reached the trapped men.

It had been a week since Keith and John began their climb into the gorge.

The rescuers brought two one-man rubber rafts, life preservers and throw-away sleeping bags. They also brought a two-way radio, climbing gear and 1,200 feet of half-inch nylon rope.

Martino's job was to find a route two half-crippled men could follow. He saw a ledge forty feet above the river. It was only a foot wide. It also sloped away from the cliff at a bad angle. John and Keith had found it, too. But they had not dared to venture out on it with their bad feet.

Martino inched along the tilted shelf. After about one hundred feet he found a rock wedged in a crevice. It was directly over the falls. He anchored a rope and returned to the trapped men. He would take them along the rope and then lower them down to the flat rock at the top of the falls.

He, Finan, and Taylor made sling seats, fastening them to the rope with snap-links. Then they started out, one at a time. Martino led. They hung onto the rope and shuffled their feet along. The dangerous river was raging close below. They pressed themselves against the cliff like human flies! In a couple of places the ledge disappeared. There they had to swing across, hand over hand, on the sagging rope. They were safe enough, as long as the rope held!

Once on the rock at the top of the falls they found the next step even more dangerous. Martino decided to let one man down on a rope. Then he would lower an inflated raft to him. The lead man would anchor two hundred feet of rope at the foot of the falls. He would swim the raft down to the rocks at the end of the pool. Then he would attach the other end of the rope there. The rest of the party would follow, one by one. They would either swim the length of the pool or ferry across it in the second raft, hanging onto the rope.

Finan went first. As he stepped out on a rock, a whirlpool caught the raft and took it down out of sight. It all happened so fast, the men watching hardly saw it. But one by one, the men made it over the falls and across the pool as planned.

Now there was a second falls to go over. Keith went first this time. He found the lost raft bobbing under the pounding falls, but he could not reach it. John handed him his fishing rod. Trying over and over again, he was able to hook the cork grip in a loop on the side. He brought it within reach and pulled it up. Then he paddled the length of the pool and put the raft in a crevice. Looking around, he tried to find a rock so he could anchor the lead rope. They were all too big.

Climbing around on the rocks, Keith came to a place where the river went straight down between three boulders. It was like a giant bathtub drain. He had to get by it. Hanging onto the rope tied one hundred feet upstream, he jumped. But his feet went out from under him on the wet and slippery shelf! He was brought up with a jerk that felt like it had torn his arms out of their sockets. He was dangling on the rope in a hole up to his waist with tons of water sucking him down!

The rest of the party could not see him and had no idea anything had gone wrong. He could not yell above the thunder of the river. So he gripped the rope, kicked and fought. Finally he got a knee up on a rock. Bracing his body he pulled himself out.

43

He never did succeed in fastening the rope to a rock. Instead he doubled it to make a loop. Then he served as a human pulley to tow the men and packs down on the second raft.

Once out of the rocks, they swam and rafted down a long, half-moon pool that ended on an open beach. It had taken six hours to go the last five hundred yards. But they were finally through the gorge.

A jet helicopter was standing by on a sandbar. John and Keith gratefully climbed aboard. The takeoff would be tricky. The big, olive-drab chopper lifted itself from the bar. Then it made a turn and flew straight at the wall. At the last second it tilted and headed for the other side. It zigzagged back and forth like a giant dragonfly all the way to the top. The two men gave a deep sigh of relief when the chopper finally cleared the rim.

The men were out of the Devil's Hole at last!

Keith and John were home before dark. Each man had lost twelve pounds. Their feet were in very bad shape, especially John's. Both men lost most of their toenails. It was eight months before Keith lost his last damaged toenail and his feet felt normal again. But no infection had set in and the healing was normal for both men.

45

They had no way of knowing it at the time, but the two trapped fishermen had been front-page news across the country. One news story said: "How they got there is unknown. How or when they will be rescued is uncertain."

The pilot who flew them out of the gorge was a hero. Capt. John S. McLeod received an air medal for his daring part in the rescue. He was also cited by the President of the United States.

Keith and John still talk about the great fishing in Devil's Hole that summer of 1962. The fish are

still there, for sure. But at least two fishermen are content to leave them there.

Neither Keith Oveson nor John McClary will ever try to go back to the Devil's Hole!

Stay on the edge of your seat.

Read:

FROZEN TERROR

DANGER IN THE AIR

MISTAKEN JOURNEY

TRAPPED IN DEVIL'S HOLE

DESPERATE SEARCH

FORTY DAYS LOST

FOUND ALIVE

GRIZZLY!

SURVIVAL

TRUE STORIES

13149

799.1
EAS

East, Ben.

Trapped in Devil's
Hole.